EZRA IN PURSUIT

THE GREAT MAZE CHASE

Join Ezra now in days of yore;
Eighteen hundred seventy-four.
The Logan Gang has struck again—
One bad woman, two bad men.
Solve the mazes! Find the loot!
Help out Ezra in pursuit!

A Doubleday Book for Young Readers

To Steve, Adam, and Kim

A Doubleday Book for Young Readers
Published by Delacorte Press
Bantam Doubleday Dell Publishing Group, Inc.
1540 Broadway, New York, New York 10036
Doubleday and the portrayal of an anchor with a dolphin are trademarks of
Bantam Doubleday Dell Publishing Group, Inc.
Copyright © 1993 by Rosalyn Schanzer

Library of Congress Cataloging in Publication Data
Schanzer, Rosalyn.
Ezra in pursuit : the great maze chase / by Rosalyn Schanzer.
p.   cm.
"A Doubleday book for young readers."
Summary: Rhyming text and illustrations, in a frontier setting, take a boy
through a series of maze puzzles, in pursuit of three robbers.
ISBN 0-385-30884-1
1. Maze puzzles—Juvenile literature. [1. Maze puzzles. 2. Puzzles.] I. Title.
GV1507.M3S33   1993   793.73—dc20   92-25815   CIP   AC

The illustrations are done in colored dyes and india ink on bristol board.
The book is set in 18-point ITC Cheltenham Book Condensed, and the
cover and title pages are set in typefaces representative of the wooden
type used in posters of the 1870s. Typography and design by
Rosalyn Schanzer and Lynn Braswell.

Manufactured in the United States of America
October 1993
10 9 8 7 6 5 4 3 2 1

"To the train...
on the double!"

Down the bed sheet, through the town,
Ezra hunts the robbers down.
Bridges! Tunnels! Rough terrain!
Chase the Logans to the train!

By handcar Ezra now must go,
Past broken tracks and buffalo.
The Logan Gang he must restrain....
They stole the safe right off the train!

Hurry on. Use common sense.
Avoid the snakes and barbed-wire fence.
The stagecoach has been robbed today.
A man says, "They went thataway!"

START HERE

Swamps and fires block Ezra's path.
These bandits have incurred great wrath!
A family farm has just been stricken.
They took two cows, six pigs, one chicken.

The Pueblo Indians are shaken—
Furs and turquoise have been taken!
The Logan Gang has up and gone.
Steadfast, Ezra hurries on.

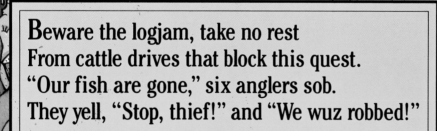

Beware the logjam, take no rest
From cattle drives that block this quest.
"Our fish are gone," six anglers sob.
They yell, "Stop, thief!" and "We wuz robbed!"

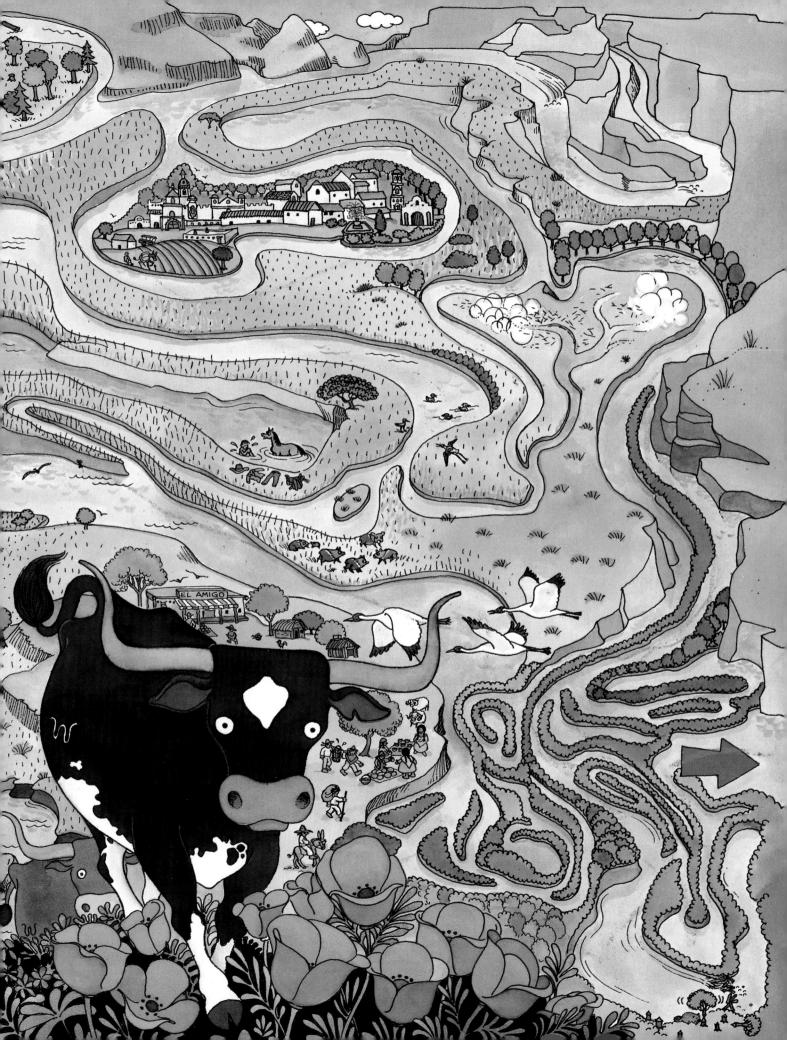

START
HERE

Help! These quetzals lost their plumes!
Through the rapids Ezra zooms!
Past many dangers he must go
While heading south through Mexico.

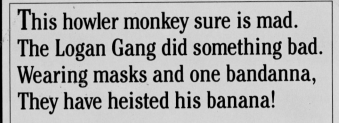

This howler monkey sure is mad.
The Logan Gang did something bad.
Wearing masks and one bandanna,
They have heisted his banana!

Not long ago, the Logans hid
In an ancient pyramid.
An age-old Aztec goddess glowers;
The bad guys stole her Prince of Flowers.

Beware of bears and vampire bats
And spiders sitting on your hats!
We're very near and closing fast—
Ezra sees the thieves at last!!!

With skill these villains won't forget,
Our hero hurls a giant net.
Oh, wicked woman, rotten men—
The thieves cry, "Curses! Foiled again!"

The Logans' victims feel great pleasure
When Ezra gives them back their treasure.
The Logan Gang is vexed and pale
As Ezra locks them up in jail.
Ezra gives the bank its booty.
"You're my hero," swoons a cutie.

JAIL

SHERIFF

"Go west, young man" was the byword of adventurers flocking to settle the American frontier in the mid-1800s. By 1874, gambling, brawling, and drinking were rampant in the boomtowns of Colorado, and banks were often robbed at gunpoint.

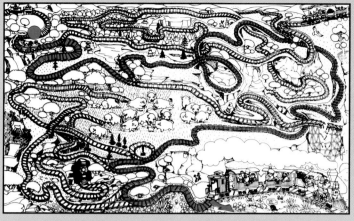

Railroads linked Denver to both coasts by 1870, and in 1873, Jesse James robbed his first train. Between 1872 and 1874, 3,700,000 buffalo were killed by white hunters, and the Plains Indians' main source of meat, clothing, and tents was gone forever.

Cries of "Pikes Peak or Bust" signaled the beginning of a series of gold and silver rushes that swelled Colorado's population between 1858 and the 1890s. Gold was so common that when President U. S. Grant visited Central City in 1873, less plentiful silver bricks were used to pave his way from street to hotel.

The Indian Wars that began in 1860 ended an era when the last magnificent Apache warriors were vanquished in 1886. Ancient Pueblo Indians had built homes in the sides of steep cliffs, and Pueblo adobe homes were made of sunbaked mud and straw. Two Pueblo villages in New Mexico have been inhabited continuously since A.D. 1100.

Tropical rain forests were still tranquil, beautiful, and vibrant with thousands of undiscovered varieties of exotic fruits, butterflies, orchids, and wild animals. Treetop canopies were so dense that the ground was totally dark even on the sunniest day.

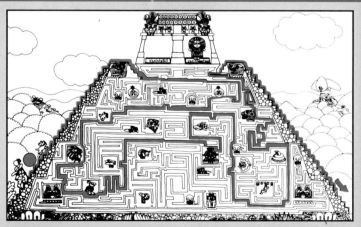

Ruins of ancient civilizations were so widespread that any nineteenth-century farm worker might turn up an artifact. Xochipilli, the Prince of Flowers, was the youthful Aztec god of love, spring, games, and dancing. He is mourned here by his wife, Xochiquetzal, or Precious Flower, the goddess of flowers, love, and beauty.

Buffalo Bill Cody appeared in the first of his rip-roaring, sharp-shooting Wild West shows in 1872. Passengers traveling in the stagecoaches that sped across the West were in constant danger of robbery.

The Homestead Act, signed by President Lincoln in 1862, promised 160 acres of land on the Great Plains to anyone who would work it for five years. Ranches spread into Colorado as a "Cattle Kingdom" took shape. Rustling led ranchers to brand their cattle, and barbed wire cut homesteads from open range.

In 1874, Billy the Kid began his criminal career as a cattle thief and killer in New Mexico, and Texas Rangers were commissioned as peace officers to fight Comanches, cattle thieves, murderers, smugglers, bank and train robbers, and mine bandits. Texas longhorns were driven north on the Chisholm Trail from near San Antonio, Texas, to Abilene, Kansas.

In Mexico in 1874, *bandidos* and guerrilla bands terrorized the countryside. Forests in the Gulf Coastal Plains were home to the elegant resplendent quetzal, a bird considered sacred by pre-Columbian Indians, who used its flowing green feathers to adorn their royalty.

The Sierra Madre del Sur is a rugged mountain range rising along the Pacific Coast in Mexico's Southern Uplands. Its caves made excellent hiding places for mother mountain lions with their cubs, blindfish, bats, and maybe even a few bank robbers!

PURSUIT ROUTE

1874

This book was rigorously researched by examining hundreds of photographs, drawings, and paintings done during the 1870s, and by studying the history, geography, folklore, plants, and animals of the period. Every detail was considered, from the wildflowers and wildlife of the shortgrass prairies to the construction of gold mines. Clothing, food, architecture, artifacts, methods of transportation and farming, and even many of the signs accurately reflect the era and places depicted.

★

Rosalyn Schanzer has illustrated hundreds of books, posters, magazine articles, games, and filmstrips for children. Mazes have always been a popular part of her repertoire. She is intrigued by the way a viewer can actually be drawn into an exotic place or time by following the paths of a maze, turning its corners, and getting lost amid a myriad of wonders, perils, and unlooked-for treasures. And researching the history of her journeys to the past is half the fun, she says.

An ardent devotee of photography, travel, swimming, and soccer, Rosalyn Schanzer lives in Fairfax Station, Virginia, with her husband, Steve, their children, Adam and Kim, and their dog, Jones.